DOCTRINE OF CLOG OF REDEMPTION

VOLUME 2, ISSUE 4 OF BRILLOPEDIA

ADITHYA NARAYANAN

Contents

Preface

"Start writing, no matter what. The water does not flow until the faucet is turned on".

- Louis L'Amour

Hundreds of students and professors are contributing their work to Brillopedia, we are here to provide ample information about Law and Contemporary issues. Our aim is to provide a platform for today's generation to express their views and ideas on law and contemporary law.

Author

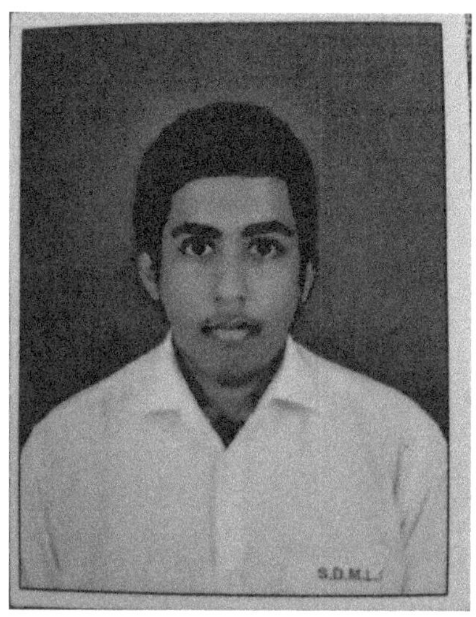

ADITHYA NARAYANAN

CHAPTER ONE

ABSTRACT

When a mortgage happens, he has the authority to retrieve his property. When he reimburses the amount of mortgage taken. This is termed the right of redemption and is derived from equity. Everything which blocks the mortgagor's right to redeem his property is void, and such hindrance accounts for a clog on the right of redemption. This is as well as called the doctrine of a clog on redemption.

Regarding a mortgage, two classes of dividends are produced. The first and foremost interest which is generated is the creditor's interest in the property. Which is restricted and provisional. The second classification is the residuary interest which perhaps is decided by subtracting the interest of the creditor or mortgagee and such interest remains with the mortgagor. Division of this interest allows the right of redemption after repayment of the loan. This authority of the mortgagor is also called the equitable right to redeem.

The right of redemption to the borrower is given under Section 60(1) of the Transfer of Property Act, of 1882. The agreement of mortgage is complete when the defaulter pays back the loan amount and practices his right to redeem the property. The right furnished under the Act is a legal right and to, implement it lawful provisions have to be adhered to. Thus, this article discusses briefly various aspects of the Clog of Redemption.

Keywords: mortgage, redemption, residuary interest, mortgagor, mortgagee, equitable right, clog.

CHAPTER TWO

INTRODUCTION

In a mortgage, the most important right possessed by the mortgagor is the right to redeem the mortgage. **Redemption** means **getting back the mortgaged property** by the mortgagor by paying back the mortgage loan money to the mortgagee. Redemption usually takes place when the mortgagor repays the mortgage money, thereby getting a right to have the property. This is known as the **right of redemption.**

In English law, the mortgagor's right to redemption is called the **'Equity of redemption**. In India, the right to redemption and equity of redemption has the same meaning. Section 60 of the Transfer of Property Act, is a statutory right.

Right of redemption is known by the maxim **'once a mortgage is always a mortgage'**. It means the right of redemption is part and parcel of the law of mortgage. It is the most important right possessed by the mortgagor. It cannot be removed by the act of parties to the mortgage.

Once the money is paid by the mortgagor, he immediately gets the right of redemption. After redemption of the mortgage, the mortgagor has the right to require the mortgagee to deliver to him the mortgage deed and other relevant documents in his possession.

Poulose and another Vs. State Bank of Travancore:

The court held that the right of redemption must be exercised by the mortgagor before the mortgagee has filed a suit for the enforcement of the mortgage. After the filing of the suit by the mortgagee, the right of redemption is no longer available to the mortgagor.

The right of redemption cannot be removed either by law or by contract, etc. this permanent right of redemption of the mortgagor is known by the maxim 'once a mortgage is always a mortgage'.

Thus, once a mortgage deed is entered, it can never be changed because such changes will affect the right of redemption. A suit for redemption can be instituted by a mortgagor, a puisne mortgagee, a sub-mortgagee, a lessee of a mortgaged property, etc.[1]

[1]*Paulose And Another v. State Bank of Travancore.*, Judgment https://www.casemine.com/judgement/in/56094e73e4b01497112812b7.

CHAPTER THREE

RIGHT OF MORTGAGOR TO REDEEM: (Sec. 60)

Section 60 reads as follows-

1. At any time after the principal money has become due, on payment of the mortgage money at a proper time and place by the mortgagor, the mortgagee is to deliver to him (the mortgagor), the mortgage deed and all documents relating to the mortgaged property which are in the possession of the mortgagee.

Further, at the cost of the mortgagor, the mortgagor may direct the mortgagee

i. To re-transfer the mortgaged property to him, or
ii. To transfer the mortgaged property to a specific third person, or
iii. If the mortgage has been affected by a registered deed, then the mortgagee must execute a registered acknowledgment in writing that all mortgagee's rights in the mortgaged property affecting the interest of the mortgagor are fully extinguished (terminated).[1]

a. **Prithi Nath Singh Vs. Suraj Ahir:**

The Court held that once the mortgage money has been paid, the mortgage comes to an end and the mortgagor has the statutory right to recover possession and if the mortgagee has the mortgaged property, then he has to deliver possession of the property to the mortgagor.[2]

a. **Singh Ram (D) through LRS Vs. Sheo Ram and Ors. (2008):**

The Supreme Court held that as per Section 62 of the Transfer of Property Act, the right to redeem continues, if no time limit is fixed, till the mortgage money is paid and as such, there is no time limit. In other cases, the right to redeem accrues on the date of entering into a mortgage agreement, resulting in the extinguishment of the right of redemption after 30 years.[3]

c. Shankar Sakharam Kenjale Vs. Narayan Krishna Gade and another (2020):

The Supreme Court held that the right to redeem a mortgage can be terminated, only by an operation known to law. In this case, the Mortgagor filed a suit for redemption of the mortgage and repossession of the land upon receipt of the mortgage money.

The Supreme Court held that the right to redemption cannot be lost except by way of the process of law. The Court observed that the right of redemption is an indispensable right to the mortgagor, even though he may, by express contract, abandon his right to redeem the property.

Equity is that a mortgage is intended only to provide security to the lender and thus any agreement which prevents redemption is void. The right of redemption cannot be extinguished.

The Judgment emphasizes the legal principle significant to all kinds of mortgages: "once a mortgage is always a mortgage".

Rules of redemption:

1. The right of redemption conferred by sec. 60 cannot be extinguished by the act of the parties or by decree of the Court. The right conferred by this section is called the 'right to redeem', and a suit to enforce it is called the 'suit for redemption.

2. If the time fixed for payment of the principal loan money has expired or no such time has been fixed, then the mortgagee is entitled to reasonable notice before payment of such money by the mortgagor and return of the property by the mortgagee.

3. If the mortgagee or mortgagees have acquired, besides other shares, the share of a mortgagor in a property, then the mortgagor is entitled to redeem his share only on payment of a proportionate part of the mortgage loan amount.

4. Only if the money is fully paid can the mortgagor redeem the property. If the money is not paid even after the due date, the mortgagee gets a right of foreclosure (i.e., the right to sell the property for default of payment). Thus, the right of redemption and foreclosure are co-extensive.[4]

CLOG (CONDITION) ON REDEMPTION:

Since the right of redemption is a statutory right, it cannot be removed by the act of the parties. 'Clog' means condition. If any condition is prescribed as so to remove the right of redemption, such condition is known as a 'clog on redemption'. A 'clog on redemption' is always null and void.

i. **Pormal Kanji Govindji Vs. Vrajla Karsandas Purohit AIR 1989 SC 436:**

The Supreme Court held that it is settled law in England and India that a mortgage cannot be made altogether irredeemable or redemption made illusory.[5]

Kinds of Clogs in Redemption:

The clog on redemption may be in any one of the following ways:

a. The mortgagor may be deprived of his right of redeeming the mortgaged property. E.g., one of the terms of the mortgage is that if the mortgagor fails to redeem the mortgage within the specified period, then the mortgagor's right in the mortgaged property ceases and the mortgage deed will become a sale deed in favor of the mortgagee. This is a clog on redemption and hence shall not be given effect.

b. The terms of the mortgage may give a benefit to the mortgagee and a corresponding burden on the mortgagor even after redemption by the mortgagor. This is a clog on redemption.

c. Generally, a long term for redemption is not a clog, but it should be weighed depending on the circumstances of each case. If the length of the term of a mortgage is oppressive and unreasonable, then it is a clog on redemption.

Fateh Mohammad Vs. Ram Dayal:

The length of the mortgage was 200 years; hence, the Court held the condition to be a clog on redemption of the mortgage.

d. If the terms of the mortgage deed deprive the mortgagor's right of redemption after a certain period, then such restriction is a clog on redemption.

e. If the condition of the mortgage postpones the redemption for default of payment (i.e., in case the mortgagor fails to pay the money on a particular date), it is a clog on redemption.

Mohammad Sher Khan Vs. Seth Swami Dayal:

The period of mortgage was for five years but in case of default by the mortgagor, the mortgagee could get possession of the property for twelve years and the mortgagor could not hold to be a clog on redemption.

f. If a condition is stipulated preventing the mortgagor from alienating the property or taking a loan on the property during the mortgage period, it is a clog on redemption.

g. If the right of redemption is available only to the mortgagor, but not to his heirs, it is a clog on redemption.

h. In case of default by the mortgagor to pay the mortgage money on a particular date, then there will be an enhanced rate of interest (for default) on the mortgage money. This amounts to a clog on redemption.[6]

1. **Murilal Vs. Devkaram:**

The Supreme Court confirmed the decisions of various High Courts on the point that 'the clause in a mortgage deed which bars redemption is like a clog on the equity of redemption. The right of a mortgagor to redeem the property cannot be taken away and restricted by a clog. If any such clause is incorporated in a mortgage deed, it is void and the Courts must ignore it.[7]

2. **Gangadhar Vs. Shankar Lal:**

The Court formulated rules for deciding a clog on redemption of the mortgage. Whether a particular transaction is a clog on the equity of redemption or not depends primarily upon the period of redemption or not depends primarily upon the period of redemption or depends primarily upon the period of redemption, the circumstances under which the mortgage was created, the economic and financial position of the mortgagor and his relationship with the mortgagee and the totality of all the circumstances under which a mortgage is created. These factors must be correlated to each other and viewed comprehensively to determine whether there are clogs in the equity of redemption or not.

The Court held that a condition converting a mortgage into a sale is invalid, as it is a clog on the equity of redemption.[8]

3. Stanley Vs. Wilde:

This is a leading case in **'Clog on Redemption'**. The Court held that any stipulation in mortgage transaction which is inconsistent with redemption is a clog on redemption and hence invalid.[9]

Collateral Advantages to the Mortgage – A Clog on Redemption:

Sometimes, in a mortgage, as per the terms of the mortgage, the mortgagee may be entitled to something in addition to more than the payment of the principal amount, interest, and cost thereof. Whether such something also amounts to a clog on redemption or not depends on the terms and circumstances of each mortgage.

The general rule is that Court will strike down if such 'something additional' is an 'oppressive bargain or unfair and unconscionable or like a penalty or inconsistent with the legal or equitable right to redeem'. Otherwise, such mortgages will be treated as valid.[10]

KREGLINGER'S RULE AND INDIAN LAW: (NOAKES Vs. RICE):

'R' mortgaged his house to one 'M'. M put a condition that R should always sell the liquors manufactured by the Noakes company only in the mortgaged premises and in no other place. This condition should exist even after the mortgage is over.

The Court held that the condition was a clog on redemption as it created an undue collateral advantage to the mortgagee, i.e., to sell all the liquors only in the mortgagor's premises and it affects the mortgagor's right of absolute enjoyment after redemption and so the condition was void after redemption of the mortgage.

The Biggs Case (1898):

The mortgagor, a hotel owner, mortgaged his hotel premises to a brewer (liquor manufacturer). In the mortgaged deed it was agreed both by the mortgagor and the mortgagee that during a mortgage period of 5 years, the mortgagee would sell the beer only to the mortgagor and the mortgagor would buy beer only from the mortgagee. The mortgagor would buy beer only from the mortgagee. The mortgagors, after 2 years, stopped buying beer from the mortgagees and hence claimed redemption of the mortgage.

The court held of Appeal held that for the mortgaged period of 5 years, the mortgagor must buy only from the mortgagee, and hence there could be no redemption before this period. The Court further held that the above condition was not a clog on redemption.

Kreglinger Vs. New Patagonia (Meat and Cola Storage Co. Ltd):

Kreligner was a firm of wool brokers. They loaned 10000 pounds to Patagonia Meat Co., which did a meat preserving business. The condition was that Patagonia Meat Co. would pay the loan back to kreglinger by giving one month's notice. The above loan to Patagonia Meat Co. was not on mortgage but by a floating charge on the meat company's movable property (stock).

There was an additional condition that for the loan period of years from the date of the loan, the meat company must not sell sheep skins to anyone other than except Kreligner firm, provided Kreligner firm paid the best price for the sheep skins.

The meat company repaid the loan in 2-1/2 years to the Kreligner firm. Now, the Kreligner firm sued the meat company for specific performance of supply of sheep skins for the balance period of 2-1/2 years.

The house of lords held that the agreement of the sale of sheep skins by the meat company to the Kreligner was not a term in the mortgage but of a collateral agreement and hence it was not a clog on redemption.

It is thus clear from the above points and case laws that 'clog on redemption is a Rule of Justice, Equity and Good Conscience and the dictum **'once a mortgage is always a mortgage'** is correct.[11]

[1]Diganth Raj Sehgal, *Critical analysis of mortgagor's right of redemption* - IPleaders (Aug. 11, 2020), https://blog.ipleaders.in/critical-analysis-mortgagors-right-redemption/.

[2]*Prithi Nath Singh and Others v. Suraj Ahir and Others*, Judgment https://www.casemine.com/judgement/in/5609ab26e4b014971140bcef.

[3]*Indiankanoon.Org*, https://indiankanoon.org/doc/116608229/.

[4]*Shankar Sakharam Kenjale (Died) Through his Legal Heir vs. Narayana Krishna Gade and anr.*, Law Times Journal (June 2, 2020), https://lawtimesjournal.in/shankar-sakharam-kenjale-died-through-his-legal-heir-vs-naryana-krishna-gade-and-anr/.

[5]*Pomal Kanji Govindji & Ors V. Vrajlal Karsandas Purohit & Ors (4)*, Asian Encyclopaedia of Law (Mar. 22, 2014), https://india.lawi.asia/pomal-

kanji-govindji-and-ors-v-vrajlal-karsandas-purohit-and-ors-4/.

[6]*Mohammad Sher Khan v. Raja Seth Swami Dayal*, Judgment https://www.casemine.com/judgement/in/56b49343607dba348f005cae.

[7]*Indiankanoon.Org*, https://indiankanoon.org/doc/1531467/.

[8]LI Network, *Seth Ganga Dhar Vs Shankar Lal and Others*, Law Insider India (Feb. 18, 2022), https://www.lawinsider.in/judgment/seth-ganga-dhar-vs-shankar-lal-and-others.

[9]*Stanley v Wilde 1899*, (July 27, 2022), https://www.lawteacher.net/cases/santley-v-wilde-1899.php.

[10]*Advantages of A Collateral Mortgage |*, Northwood Mortgage (Sept. 30, 2014), https://www.northwoodmortgage.com/mortgage-questions/advantages-collateral-mortgage/.

[11]Vivek Singh, *Doctrine of clog on redemption*, (Mar. 27, 2015), https://www.lawctopus.com/academike/doctrine-of-clog-on-redemption/.

CHAPTER FOUR

EXERCISE OF RIGHT OF REDEMPTION

Before Redemption:

The mortgagor can exercise his right of redemption in the following three ways:

1. By paying the mortgage money to the mortgagee out of Court.

a. **Nijalingappa Vs. Chanbasawa:**

The Bombay High Court held that in a redemption suit, a mortgagee can recover from his mortgagor the reasonable and proper costs incurred in making permanent improvements, viz., making the property more productive; in allowing costs of improvements, the court must guard against extravagant or unfounded claims and it should inquire strictly into the bona fides and fairness of the claim in each particular case.[1]

ii. Ramappa Vs. Yellapa:

The Court held that as the amount spent on improvements was five times the mortgage amount the claim was found unreasonable and hence not allowed.

1. By depositing the mortgaged money in the Court
2. By filing a suit for redemption of the mortgage.

After Redemption:

After redemption, the mortgagor has the following rights:

1. Right to get back the mortgage deed and other documents of title of the mortgaged property.
2. Possession of the mortgaged property.
3. Acknowledgement from the mortgagee that he has received the mortgaged loan amount from the mortgagor.

Extinguishment of Right of Redemption:

The mortgagor's right of redemption is extinguished in the following three ways:

1. By foreclosure, i.e., Sale through Court
2. Mortgagee exercising the power of sale.
3. When the mortgage becomes barred by limitation under Limitation Act (12 years).
4. By mutual agreement between mortgagor and mortgagee.
5. By operation of law like a merger, statutory provisions, etc.[2]

The doctrine of consolidation:

The doctrine of consolidation is an English Doctrine. Consolidation means the right of the mortgagor who holds several mortgages executed by the same mortgagor to require the simultaneous redemption of all mortgages.

1. Consolidation can now be claimed only if an express contract stipulates such a right.
2. The right of consolidation can be enforced only when the mortgagee for several mortgages is the same person.
3. Only if the mortgages have been originally made by the same mortgagor, the right of consolidation exists.
4. E.g., A borrows Rs. 5,00,000/- from B in 2000 on a usufructuary mortgage for 10 years. In 2005, A borrows a further sum of Rs. 3,00,000/- from B and executes a separate document promising to repay within 5 years. The deed provides that without repaying the second unsecured debt A cannot redeem the usufructuary mortgage. Now, this contract between the mortgagor and the mortgagee is for the consolidation of unsecured debt with mortgage debt. This is not permissible.[3]

RULE AGAINST PARTIAL REDEMPTION (Sec. 61):

The Doctrine of consolidation is also known as the 'Rule against partial redemption' which is incorporated in Sec. 61 of the Transfer of Property Act.

Section 61 reads: -

A mortgagor who has executed two or more mortgages in favor of the same mortgagee, and when the principal money of any two or more of the mortgages has become due, the mortgagor is entitled to redeem any one such mortgage separately, or any two or more of such mortgages together.

The mortgagor's right of redemption should be exercised in respect of the whole property and should not be exercised in parts. A part owner or the purchaser of part equity of redemption cannot redeem his share alone. He can only redeem the entire mortgage.

There is one exception to the above rule. The mortgage security is split up if the mortgagee acquires a share in the mortgaged property by sale or inheritance. Piecemeal redemption is possible.[4]

PERSONS WHO MAY SUE FOR REDEMPTION: (Sec. 91)

Besides the mortgagor, any of the following persons may redeem or institute a suit for the redemption of the mortgaged property-

a. Any person who has any interest in or charges upon the property mortgaged.
b. Any surety for the payment of the mortgage debt.
c. In a suit for the administration of the mortgagor's estate, any creditor of the mortgagor who has obtained a decree for the sale of the mortgaged property.[5]

PROHIBITION OF TACKING: (Section 93)

Section 93 of the Transfer of Property Act reads-

Even if a subsequent mortgagee pays off a prior mortgage, whether with or without notice to an intermediate mortgagee, he cannot acquire any priority in respect of his original security.

The effect is that a third mortgagee paying off the first mortgage loan acquires priority over the intermediate mortgagees' redemption in respect of the first mortgage but not concerning his mortgage.

E.g., A mortgages his house to B and then to C and then to D. now, D can redeem the mortgage from C and B. Similarly, C can redeem from B. But B cannot redeem from C and D. Similarly, C cannot redeem from D.

So, the rule is – when there are several mortgages, the latter mortgagee can always redeem the earlier mortgages but the earlier mortgagee cannot redeem the latter mortgages. However, this is possible with the consent of the other mortgagees concerned.[6]

'RIGHT OF REDEEMING CO-MORTGAGOR' TO EXPENSE: (Section 95)

When one of several mortgagors redeems the mortgaged property, he can enforce his right of subrogation under Section 92 against his co-mortgagors.

Further, the mortgagor redeeming the property is entitled to add (to the mortgage money recoverable from other co-mortgagors) such proportion of the expenses properly incurred by him in such redemption.[7]

[1]*Indiankanoon.Org*, https://indiankanoon.org/doc/1977294/.

[2]*Redemption Rights Clause*, Overview, How to Exercise, Types (Jan. 5, 2020), https://corporatefinanceinstitute.com/resources/commercial-real-estate/redemption-rights-clause/.

[3]Keith Robinson, *Ireland: The Application of The Equitable Doctrine of Consolidation - AIB Mortgage Bank V O'Toole*, Charges, Mortgages, Indemnities (May 1, 2018),

[4]Gautam Badlani, *Right of Redemption Under Transfer of Property Act: An Analysis*, (Feb. 20, 2007), https://www.lawyersclubindia.com/articles/right-of-redemption-under-transfer-of-property-act-an-analysis-14638.asp.

[5]*Ons Who May Sue for Redemption*, Section 91 of Transfer of Property Act, 1882: Pers (Feb. 11, 2015), https://ibclaw.in/section-90-persons-who-may-sue-for-redemption/.

[6]*The Doctrine of Tacking under the Transfer of Property Act* - IPleaders (Mar. 8, 2021), https://blog.ipleaders.in/doctrine-tacking-transfer-property-act/.

[7]https://legislative.gov.in/sites/default/files/A1882-04.pdf.

CHAPTER FIVE

CONCLUSION

To conclude, a clog on redemption is an entity that cannot be governed absolutely. The clog must be resolved through immediate examination of the mortgage deed. Thus, the doctrine of clog on redemption is conditional to disapproval also. This doctrine observes the individual party as the only sufferer. Both parties are based on risk and they need to be secured also. As this doctrine concentrates on the only individual party, it is opposed to public law. This model gives one party a defense to get away from his duty is bad law to regulate. In our Country India, the absolute choice is provided to the Court to determine as to which circumstances create the part of clog.